BOSS
BETTINA

Our sister Bettina is bossy.

Whenever we play hopscotch,
Bettina always has to go first.

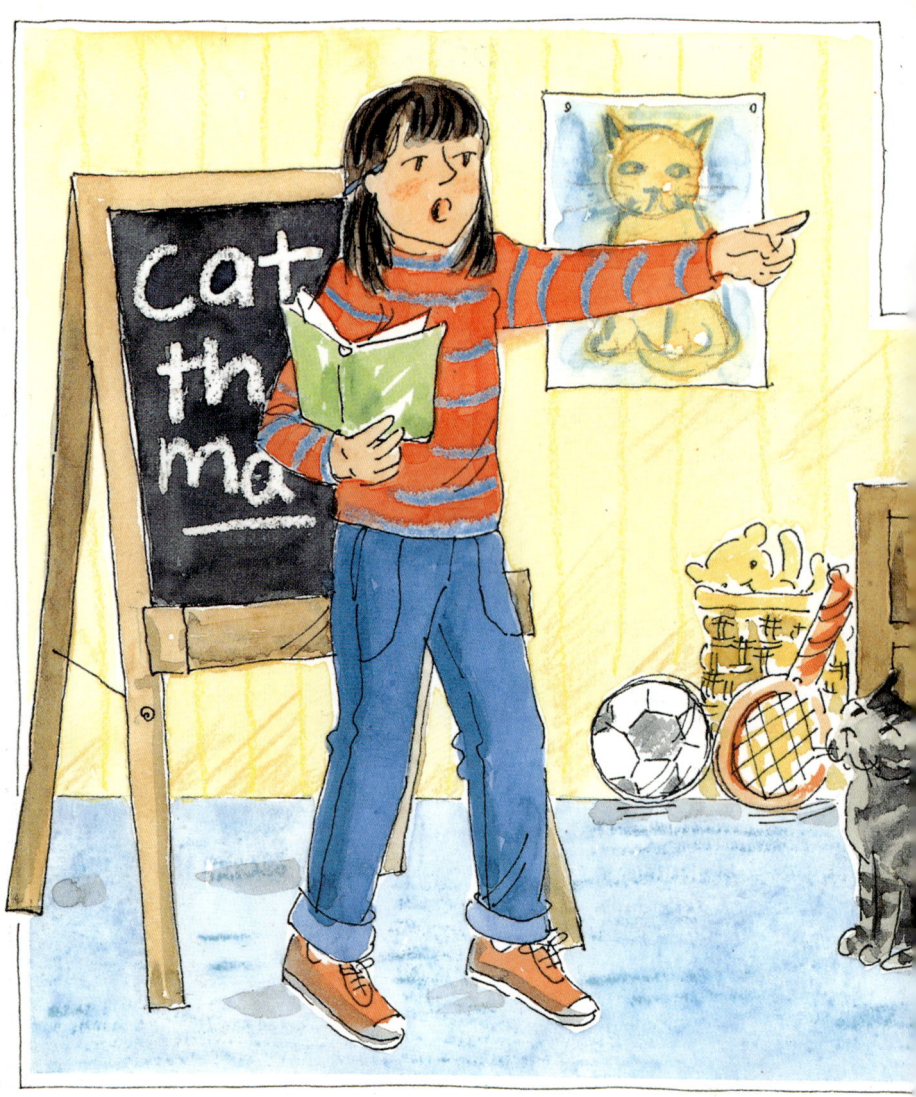

Whenever we play school, Bettina always has to be the teacher.

Whenever we play dress up, Bettina always has to have the best clothes.

One day we decided
that we'd had enough,
and we worked out a plan.

The next time we played hopscotch, we told Bettina our new rules.

"Okay," said Bettina.
"But *I'm* going to choose first."

Our sister Bettina *is* bossy.
But she doesn't always win!